D1191752

P 8 22
STRAND PRICE
$ 5.00

PORTRAIT OF
SKYE

JOHN BAILEY

Photography by John and Tina Bailey

HALSGROVE

First published in Great Britain in 2009

Copyright © John Bailey 2009

Photography by John & Tina Bailey

All rights reserved. No part of this publication may be reproduced,
stored in a retrieval system, or transmitted in any form or by any
means without the prior permission of the copyright holder.

British Library Cataloguing-in-Publication Data
A CIP record for this title is available from the British Library

ISBN 978 1 84114 934 9

HALSGROVE
Halsgrove House,
Ryelands Industrial Estate,
Bagley Road, Wellington, Somerset TA21 9PZ
Tel: 01823 653777   Fax: 01823 216796
email: sales@halsgrove.com

Part of the Halsgrove group of companies
Information on all Halsgrove titles is available at: www.halsgrove.com

Printed and bound by Grafiche Flaminia, Italy

Contents

LOCATION MAP – Skye

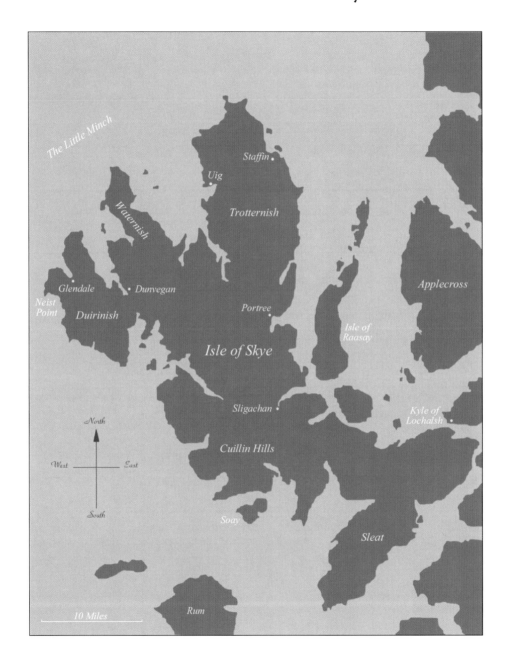

Acknowledgements

Ihave to thank Tina for contributing many of the photographs to *Portrait of Skye* and for her commitment on the many journeys, sometimes in the teeth of the most severe of winter storms, and inspiration for some of the compositions. To Nick for the photographs on pages 60 and 61. The map grid references, heights and spelling of mountain names have all been obtained from Ordnance Survey Memory Map Northern Scotland. To Angus & Teresa at the Stein for the internal photographs of the bar area and more so for accommodation on several occasions before having a base on Skye and in particular in January 2005 when due to one of the most severe storms to hit the Western Isles for decades we were well looked after despite no electricity for the week.

I would also like to thank Steven Pugsley at Halsgrove for giving me the opportunity to have *Portrait of Skye* published.

Acknowledgement should also go to the Isle of Skye with its unique landscape and ever changing light giving inspiration to all that visit.

Shells at the Coral Beaches.

Introduction

Speed bonnie boat like a bird on the wing, Onward the sailors cry
Carry the lad that's born to be king, over the sea to Skye

This Scottish folk song is about the escape of Bonnie Prince Charlie over the sea to Skye, after his defeat at Culloden in 1746. The author of the song is unknown. Skye is the largest of the Inner Hebrides with a coastline of over three hundred miles and is made up of more than a dozen long sea lochs, the effect being that nowhere on Skye are you ever more than five miles from the sea.

This book is a portrait of Skye that may help you decide to come and spend time on this wonderful island off the west coast of Scotland or be a permanent reminder of time that has been rewardingly spent on Skye and what a beautiful and magical place it is. It could just allow you to take a look and admire from afar.

It is essentially focused on the north west of the island taking you from Waterstein Head with dramatic cliffs of almost 1000 ft above Moonen Bay and on to Glendale. Continuing the journey along the shores of Loch Dunvegan passing Dunvegan Castle and on to the Coral Beaches that on a sunny day give the appearance of being a tropical island with the bright white sands set against the deep blue sea. On to Waternish then taking a brief glimpse of other areas including Trotternish with the strange and fascinating geological features of the ridge, Sligacan and the Cuillin Hills with several Munros *(summit above 3000 ft)* as a dramatic backdrop ending with some spectacular Skye sunsets.

It is not a history or geography book as many detailed books on those subjects have already been written; instead it is a journey in pictures. Brief notes are included of the areas to give a feel of past and present and how instances in time have affected the island, in particular past clan battles and the infamous Highland Clearances. It is the dramatic scenery Skye has to offer and the constantly changing moods of the weather and the light that will live long in your memory. It leaves one with a constant desire to visit and return.

General weather conditions have been noted on occasions but what you can't see are the winds that can be quite an amazing experience particularly on some exposed coasts and hills. The weather always needs to be considered before setting out, particularly on the coastal stretch between Waterstein Head, Neist and Milovaig.

However you visit, by ferry, bridge or through the pages of the book I am sure that coming over the sea to Skye will be a rewarding and worthwhile journey.

Loud the wind howls, loud the waves roar, Thunderclaps rend the air
Baffled our foes, stand by the shore, Follow they will not dare

Though the waves heave, soft will ye sleep, Ocean's a royal bed
Rocked in the deep, Flora will keep, Watch by your weary head

Waterstein Head to Neist Point

The Duirinish coast has been described as having some of the most dramatic cliff scenery in the British Isles in particular the stretch of coast between Waterstein Head and Neist Point. The Duirinish peninsula is largely uninhabited but this has not always been the case. The single track road that runs from Glendale through Borrodale and on to Ramasaig extends as a rough track to Lorgill some 2 miles further south where the remains of several croft houses can still be seen.

This area was once inhabited and was home to ten families who were subjected to the Highland Clearances. In August 1830 the crofters were ordered to leave their homes and marched to Loch Snizort a journey of up to 20 miles to be transported over seas to Nova Scotia. The croft houses were burnt to the ground and the land was given over to sheep and their tenant farmers by the generally absentee landlords. The clearances that had begun during the previous century continued well into the nineteenth century and transformed the Highland landscape to that we know and recognise today.

Waterstein Head stands over 970 ft above Moonen Bay with distant views to the west across The Little Minch to the Outer Hebrides over 20 miles distant. Inland can be seen Macleod's Tables and on a clear day extending to the Cuillin Hills. Moonen Bay was once fished by Gavin Maxwell author of *Ring Of Bright Water* for basking sharks from his base on the small island of Soay off the south of Skye close to the Cuillin Hills.

The view from Waterstein Head provides a panorama of the whole of Neist including the lighthouse and Neist Point, being the most westerly part of Skye. It has been said that Neist Point is the most westerly part of mainland Britain that can be reached by road and on foot now that the bridge is in place being further west than Lands End in Cornwall.

The lighthouse was completed in 1909 and manned right up until 1990. The light is the equivalent of 480,000 candles and has a nominal range of 16 miles but it is said to be seen for over 20 miles. There is no road access to the lighthouse for the final part of the journey, with provisions being winched down from the top of the escarpment at the end of the road. The lighthouse has to withstand the worst that nature can produce as the most severe of Atlantic winter storms first make landfall on Skye at Neist Point.

The triangulation pillar is well fenced in, but at 970 ft and a sheer
drop to Moonen Bay below perhaps not a bad thing.

Left:
Early evening in March and a tanker journeys through The Little Minch.
In the foreground Waterstein Head, the deep waters of Moonen Bay,
Neist Point with its lighthouse and beyond to the Outer Hebrides.
Viewed from the single track no through road that leads from Borrodale to Ramasaig.

Looking south along the Duirinish coast to Ramasaig Bay and The Hoe on an overcast day with the deserted crofts of Lorgill beyond but not visible from this point.

Neist Point jutting out into Moonen Bay is the most westerly part of Skye
with the peak of An t-Aigeach a sheer drop of 230 ft to the sea below.

The upper reaches of Waterstein Head reveal just how steeply the cliff face drops away from the summit. The rocks of An Stac jut out into the sea 970 ft below.

Above:
Almost a Christmas card scene on the slopes of
Beinn Charanac en route to Waterstein Head.

Right:
During autumn the hill is home to a huge
variety of Wax Cap fungi with colours ranging
from scarlet to lemon-yellow.

South Uist's highest peaks Beinn Mhor and Hecla which appear remarkably
close on a clear day are in fact 22 miles distant.

The route to Waterstein Head provides breathtaking views and none more than to Neist Point.

A snow storm sweeping in across The Little Minch from the North Atlantic.
Waterstein Head is just visible beyond the escarpment.

Completing the panorama. The scattered settlement of Waterstein overlooks
Loch Mor about to be hit by one of two heavy snow storms sweeping in. Viewed from the
small gravel parking area used for the ascent of Waterstein Head.

Waterstein Head towering above Moonen Bay on a stormy October day, seen from the single track road that leads to Neist Point.

Moonen Bay. The rocks of An Stac at the foot of Waterstein Head, Ramasaig Cliff falling steeply to Ramasaig Bay, The Hoe and, in the far distance, Mull and the west coast of Scotland.

Moonen Bay. This time a perfect day in late spring, sunny with light on-shore breezes.

Left:
Above Loch Mor again on the road from Milovaig
where the route to Waterstein Head begins.

The path to Neist Point from the escarpment with the unmistakable feature of An t-Aigeach.
The telegraph poles seen following the path take the most severe battering from Atlantic storms.

The path to Neist Point passes An t-Aigeach known as the Stallion's Head. This sheer craggy cliff face presents some of the most challenging rock climbing on Skye. A haven for gannets as can be seen dotted on the cliff face.

The spectacular escarpment on the route to Waterstein Head. 970 ft below are the
rocks of An Stac and the deep waters of Moonen Bay.

A light dusting of snow covers the ground this time down close to An t- Aigeach with
the massive outcrop of Waterstein Head dominating the scene.
The cliffs of Ramasaig glisten in the sun reflected from the water running from the marshy area
above fed by Loch Eishort. The highest point on Ramasaig Cliff is 790 ft. Inland are the higher peaks of
Beinn na Coinnich just over 820 ft and Ben Vratabreck just short of 1000 ft.

Neist Point forms part of the Glendale estate and shares in the common grazing rights for Waternish. The lighthouse buildings are privately owned and no access is available to the lighthouse. The walk to Neist Point has not always been straightforward as previous owners restricted access to the path from the road, but all is well now for a thoroughly enjoyable bracing walk. A local heating engineer Dave told me how he had worked on the accommodation at the lighthouse when it was being converted. Every day he had to walk from the top of the escarpment before he could start work and walk back up after he had finished, as there is no vehicular route to Neist Point.

The sheer cliff face of An t-Aigeach can be clearly seen from this vantage point on the shore. In the far distance on the escarpment top right are the buildings where the single track road ends and the path to Neist Point begins.

Waterstein Head from the shore at Neist.

Right:
Views across Moonen Bay to Ramasaig Cliff and The Hoe.

A close look at life in a rock pool on the shores of Neist. The sea anemones are carnivorous marine animals that cling to the rocks.

Right:
The waters around Neist Point are abundant with wildlife but also provide a spectacular sight when storms sweep in from the Atlantic.

Left:
In January 2005 the general lighthouse authorities came to a conclusion that the fog signal had a significantly reduced role in the modern marine environment due to the use of electronic position finding aids and radar. They took the decision that all fog horns were to be turned off, the last falling silent in October 2005. Fog horns were first introduced to Scotland in 1876. When fog or mist rises the light becomes less visible and from a distance unseen. As with the light for identification, the sound from the fog horn was unique to the location.

Far left:
The lighthouse with the now silent fog horn. The steep cliff face of An t-Aigeach towers above.

Left:
The fascinating rock formations worn
smooth by the constant battering from the sea.

Right:
Neist Point lighthouse stands
62 feet high, the light being 142 feet
above the sea. Built in 1909 it was
fully manned right up until 1990.

The sheer cliff face of An t-Aigeach towers 230 feet above the sea. The cliff top walk over Mointeach nan Tarbhin in the distance. The only way back to the road is a steep walk up to the escarpment from this point but a good excuse for a rest on the climb up the steep steps is to look back and marvel at the panorama of Neist set out below and onward to the outer isles.

Neist as the storm clouds gather, providing a dramatic reflection on the sea, the curve of the horizon clearly visible.

Map of Neist to Glendale

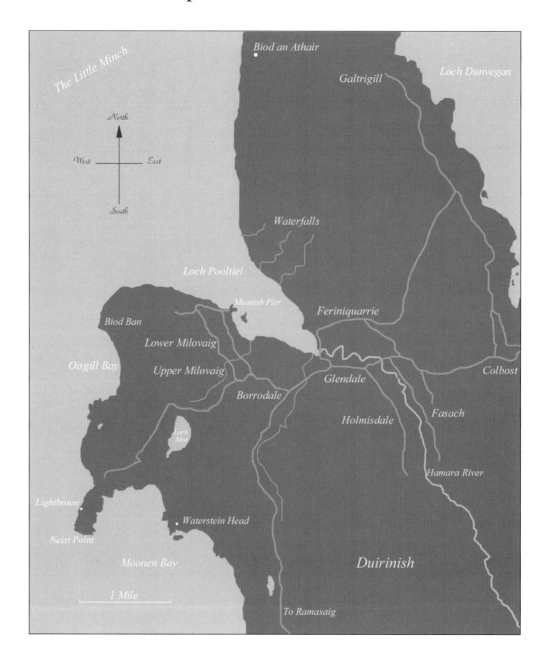

Neist to Glendale

Glendale sits north of Dunvegan reached only by the single track road that follows the shores of Loch Dunvegan for most of the 10 mile scenic journey. Glendale is made up from what are known as townships, these being the small scattered settlements of Fasac, Feriniquarrie, Holmisdal, Lephin, Lower and Upper Milovaig and Waterstein.

The Glendale estate covers 23,000 acres with its boundaries of Dunvegan in the east, Orbost in the south and The Little Minch in the west. The Glendale estate was born through the actions of crofters who under threat of the Highland Clearances instigated an uprising in 1882 led by John MacPherson. A Royal Navy gun boat landed at Meanish Pier to arrest and imprison him. His actions encouraged others and eventually in 1886 Gladstone's government passed the Crofters Holding Act that gave crofters security of tenure.

Glendale beach is at the head of Loch Pooltiel where the Hamara river flows into the sea having risen some 6 miles and 938 ft up on the slopes of Beinn a Chapuill. Meanish Pier jutting out into Loch Pooltiel is a small working harbour. A ruined watermill is evidence of past industry at Glendale beach where the islanders used water power to mill their flour.

The wildlife of the loch is varied with minke whales, seals and otters all being spotted. The tall cliffs of Biod Dubh with its many waterfalls provide a spectacular backdrop especially when viewed from the coast below Milovaig where access to the shoreline is easily obtained. During stormy weather and particularly after heavy rain the waterfalls are literally blown back up the cliffs producing a fascinating spectacle.

Glendale today is popular with tourists as the only route to Waterstein Head and Neist Point, a further 3 miles west, runs through Glendale. Many of the croft houses now serve as holiday accommodation for the growing tourist industry that caters for people seeking a holiday where you can find space and solitude amongst magnificent scenery.

Hot and cold running water near Neist.

Right:
Neist Point lighthouse from the cliff track above Oisgill Bay. The effect of storm force winds on the sea gives the impression of a light mist covering Neist on a bright sunny day.

An t-Aigeach seen towering above the lighthouse, from the vantage point a
short walk from the car park at the end of the road from Glendale.

A short distance from the old look-out is a spectacular 360 ft drop to the sea below.

The small lochan on Mointeach nan Tarbh with the sheer cliffs of Biod Ban rising 600 ft from Oisgill Bay

Right:
The coastline of Loch Pooltiel below Lower Milovaig is indented with waterfalls, caves and is a good vantage point to watch the wildlife of the loch. Here have been spotted minke whales, grey seals, otter and occasional puffins.

A wintry shower sweeps into Loch Pooltiel whipping up the sea and making it hard to distinguish between the sleet and the sea spray.

Across Loch Pooltiel from Lower Milovaig the cliffs rise abruptly from the sea culminating at Biod an Athair
a sheer drop of 1000 ft with the closer peak of Ben Skriaig at 990 ft appearing far higher from this location.
The main waterfall opposite cascades 300 ft and is one of several that appear after heavy rain.

The effect of the tidal action can be clearly seen at the base of these cliffs below Milovaig, taking on a smooth almost glass-like appearance.

Meanish Pier was once a busy port with steamers bringing coal and supplies to the area along with cattle boats arriving from North Uist. The journey continued on a drovers' track, being the only route from Glendale to the rest of Skye before the construction of the single track road from Dunvegan. Now a small working harbour for the farm fishing industry and the recent location for a leading car manufacturer's advertising campaign.

Above Loch Pooltiel are the small settlements of Upper and Lower Milovaig. Lower Milovaig is in fact higher with magnificent views out over Loch Pooltiel and across The Little Minch to the Outer Hebrides. The Glendale martyr John MacPherson lived at Milovaig. Miolabhaig is thought to be Norse for 'bay at the narrow field'.

Right:
A new day dawns in early winter.

The scattered croft houses of Lower Milovaig overlook Loch Pooltiel and on to the Outer Hebrides. Some now serve as holiday cottages to accommodate tourists to this remote, rugged and beautiful corner of North West Skye.

Right:
Puffin Cottage, a typical holiday cottage at Lower Milovaig.

The tall cliffs that rise abruptly from Loch Pooltiel are punctuated with several waterfalls that provide a spectacular sight after heavy rains, with the water being blown backward up the cliffs during stormy weather. Only inhabited by sheep. The highest point is Biod an Athair, with cliffs over 1000 ft and a sheer drop to the sea.

The waterfalls in full flow and the loch taking the full force of storm force winds and driving rain, all making for a magnificent sight. If only you could feel the wind which makes it almost impossible to walk at times. The Outer Hebrides are not visible when storms sweep in from the north west making for constantly changing scenery.

The byre. A common sight throughout Skye, now little used and falling into disrepair.

Right:
The coastline below Lower Milovaig provides access to Loch Pooltiel and rewards you with distant views
to the Outer Hebrides. Meanish Pier, the small working harbour, can be seen jutting out into the loch.

The uninhabited expanse of Biod an Athair 1000ft above the sea is known as Skye Cliff. The walk to the highest point Biod an Athair is best begun at Galtrigill at the end of the single track road leading from Colbost through Husabost. The walk is over grassy, sometimes boggy, terrain with the descent around Dunvegan Head.

Right:
The calm after the storm. Early morning January 2005, the day after one of the most severe storms to hit the Hebrides for many years. All is peaceful now as the sunlight reflects on the swollen river on its journey to the sea, flowing under the single track road at Borrodale School. Rising on the slopes of Beinn nan Corrafidheag 2 miles south, flowing just a short distance from here to Loch Pooltiel, but a fall in height of 840 feet from source to sea.

The monument on the Glendale road to commemorate the Glendale Martyrs.

To commemorate
the achievements of
The Glendale Land Leaguers
1882–1886
Locus where 600 challenged
the government forces
Imprisoned
John MacPherson the Glendale Martyr
Rev D. Maccallum Donald Macleod
John Morrison

From this point on the Glendale road near Hamaramore, the headland culminating in Biod an Athair
takes on a decidedly different aspect, as the outline of the cliff tops are more defined.
The true extent of the summit becomes more visible in this view.

The Hamara river rises below the slopes of Beinn a Chapuill at a height of 938 ft
meandering for over 6 miles through Glendale to Loch Pooltiel.

From the beach at Glendale looking toward Lower Milovaig.

Right:
Glendale beach looking along the loch out to The Little Minch and beyond to the outer isles. The calm sea reflecting the early morning sunlight. The rock in the foreground has taken on an almost giant mouse appearance – could it be the Loch Pooltiel monster? I went back a few hours later to find it had gone, but suspect that was something to do with the tide.

The post office and stores at Glendale on a rather damp and misty day.
Skye is sometimes referred to as the misty isle.

Right:
Glendale became famous in the early 1900s when crofters became freeholders of the land they worked and lived upon. The Glendale Martyrs had campaigned for decades to achieve their aim and some endured imprisonment during the late 1880s, among them the leader John Macpherson, commemorated by the monument on the road to Glendale. The Hamara river can be seen meandering through Glendale to Loch Pooltiel. Lower Milovaig can be seen in the distance with Glendale beach and the small settlement around the post office and stores at Glendale.

Map of Loch Dunvegan

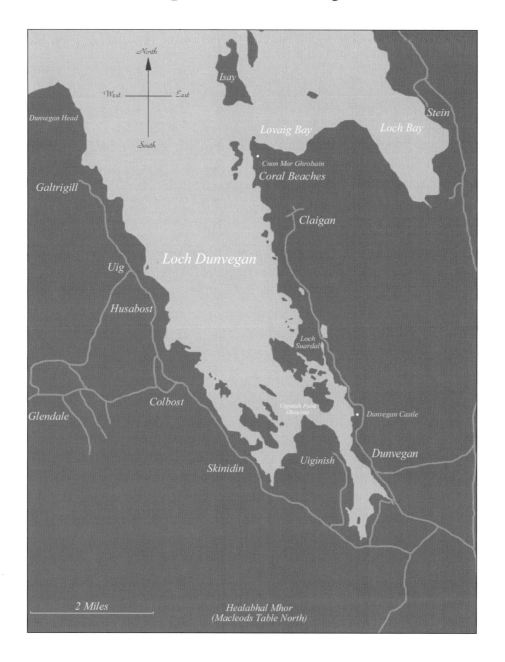

Loch Dunvegan

A tranquil sea loch that stretches from Dunvegan to the tall cliffs of Dunvegan Head, Loch Dunvegan is home to Dunvegan Castle and boasts magnificent and varied scenery along the 16 miles of shoreline culminating on the northern shore at the Coral Beaches.

The only road from Dunvegan to Glendale follows close to the western shore whilst a road to Claigan follows the eastern shore. At Claigan are the souterrain, remains of underground prehistoric structures, earth houses that are found on the Western Atlantic coast. Their exact use is unknown but thought to have been used for food storage, cattle shelters or refuge against attack. Further examples can be found on Trotternish.

Dunvegan Castle is Scotland's oldest inhabited castle, being the seat of Clan Macleod for over 800 years. Built on an almost vertical massive rock 30ft high rising from Loch Dunvegan, it is clear to see how the castle remained secure against the enemies of Clan Macleod and had the added benefit of a fresh water well.

The shoreline provides an excellent opportunity to view seals basking on the shoreline of the numerous islets, and otters too, although the waters need to be calm to give the best chance to view these elusive creatures. On the western shore near Colbost is the world famous Three Chimneys restaurant.

The single track roads of this area are largely unfenced and motorists have to be wary not only of sheep but Highland Cattle that graze the roadsides. Driving on single track roads require a degree of awareness as passing places are provided to allow safe passage. The idea being that both vehicles should adjust their speed when approaching so as to meet at the same time and then both continue at best speed.

Skye is made up of more than a dozen long sea lochs with the result that nowhere on Skye are you more than 5 miles from the sea. This also makes distances between two points something of an anomaly. The distance from Lovaig Bay just beyond the Coral Beaches to Stein on the Waternish peninsula is only 2.5 miles across Loch Bay but the journey by road back through Dunvegan is over 14 miles. This is mirrored in many locations on Skye making for some truly scenic coastal journeys.

Loch Dunvegan. Taken from the western shore near Colbost on an overcast day. Across the loch can be seen the bright white sands of the Coral Beaches, the small island of Lampay and the larger island of Isay. Ardmore Point on the Waternish peninsula can be seen beyond with the tall mountains of Harris on the horizon some 30 miles away. The distance from here to the Coral Beaches across the loch is 3 miles but the journey by road around the shores of the loch is over 10 miles.

The snow-capped Cuillins from the single track road at Colbost. Snow usually dusts the
tops in October and can linger on some of the higher north-facing summits until early June.

This specimen has withstood the ravages of the weather and the grazing of sheep. Although looking somewhat wind-blown this is a typical tree growth in a coastal location.

Left:
Early morning Loch Dunvegan with the distant Cuillin Hills silhouetted. The coastline of Loch Dunvegan is a relatively low lying area compared to the taller cliffs of Moonen Bay and Loch Pooltiel, but no less spectacular. A stunning tranquil sea loch with panoramic views across the loch and outstanding views inland to Macleod's Tables and the distant Cuillin Hills.

Colbost Croft Museum. The main feature is the croft house, now complete as it would have been and known as a black house. This one has a central chimney, whereas some would have had nothing: the smoke was allowed to find its own way out from the continuously burning peat fire, thus engulfing the house. Of the two smaller houses here, one was said to be used as an illicit still the other for storage. Several agricultural implements are also on view, some their use unknown.

Left:
Colbost Croft Museum.

Driving these roads brings back memories of a bye-gone era but requires thought and concentration. There are usually plenty of passing places and these are marked with a sign, but unless you want to make yourself very unpopular you have to remember that these are passing and not parking places.

The trick on single track roads is to drive with a combination of consideration and assertiveness. In an ideal world, vehicles approaching one another should adjust their speeds so as to meet at a passing place. That way neither waits for the other, and both proceed at best speed.

The majority of single track roads are unfenced with sheep and cattle at the side and on the road. Particular care is needed if you see a sheep on one side of the road and a lamb on the other. Nine times out of ten the lamb will run across the road to join its mother!

Right:
A glorious sunrise creating a calm scene over Loch Dunvegan close to the world famous Three Chimneys restaurant with the distant hills and mountains taking on a purple hue.

You have to get up early to catch the post. The red post box creates a striking feature in contrast to the surroundings. Note the flap on the opening to protect the contents from the elements.

Right:
A bitter cold day with a light dusting of snow on the higher ground beyond Uiginish Beacon. The wintry showers give an icy cool blue appearance to the loch. The beacon tower is a plain structure 16 feet high. The light flashes white, red, green every three seconds and can be seen for up to 7 miles.

A friendly pair posing for a portrait.

Left:
The main inhabitants of Skye enjoy a forage on the shores of Loch Dunvegan.
In the top left of the picture you can just spot the first wind farm on Skye set
high up on the slopes of Ben Aketil.

Wintry sun setting over Dunvegan with smoke rising from the peat fires of the houses below. The higher ground beyond looking like a Macleod's Table is in fact Cnoc Beag a mere 270 ft with the Cuillin Hills in the far distance.

The ruined church at Dunvegan with the Millennium Stone set high above. Dunvegan was once a main port to the Western Isles in the 1890s with the last steamers departing in the 1950s.

Duirinish Millennium Stone. The stone was taken from the shore of Strathaird and erected by the people of Dunvegan to mark the year 2000. Standing fifteen feet high and weighing five tons it was erected using the same techniques that would have been used thousands of years ago, being brought by boat and erected using manpower and wooden A frames.

Right:
Macleod's Table North. The flat topped mountain of Healabhal Mhor over 1350 ft with Loch Dunvegan
below provides the perfect backdrop for the Millennium Stone as the winter sun begins to set.

The two summits of Macleod's Table North and Macleod's Table South dominate the landscape of Duirinish. Macleod's Table North seen here from Dunvegan. The escarpment close to Garrachan on the opposite shore stands just over 160 ft high, a mere hill in comparison to the higher regions of Duirinish.

Left:
Viewed from Dunvegan, the flat topped Healabhal Mhor over 1530 ft and the smaller looking Healabhal Bheag over 1600 ft give an appearance of being sliced off by a giant and legend claims just that. It is said that they were sliced off to provide a bed and table for St Columba.

Dunvegan Castle. Loch Dunvegan, flat calm on a crisp winter's day, perfect for spotting otters should you be lucky enough to do so. The waters of the head of the loch are just visible in the distance.

Winter scene over the loch to Macleod's Tables. Another legend has it that the Ninth Chief of the Macleods wanted to impress Lords of the King's Court from Edinburgh. He invited them to a banquet at his 'room more lofty and a table more spacious' than they had, taking them to the flat topped summit with light provided by his clansman holding aloft flaming torches. The Lords were said to have been very impressed and spent time at Dunvegan Castle.

The snow capped plateaux of Healabhal Mhor and Healabhal Bheag portray
a wintry scene on a cold overcast day with frequent wintry showers.

Left:
Dunvegan Castle. Some parts date back to the 1200s. It is the ancestral home of Clan Macleod.

Highland cattle are a hardy breed that thrive where no other cattle could. They have the ability to make the best of poor grazing, are never housed and have their calves outside. They make great mothers breeding up to eighteen years but are seldom handled and although normally docile should not be put in a position that could make them react. Cattle do not mix well with dogs and you should never try to touch them or come between mother and calf.

Left:
Low light reflecting on the loch enhancing the tranquil scene.

The road to Claigan and the Coral Beaches passes over the small Loch Suardal, a calm and tranquil place.
At Claigan are the remains of a souterrain, an underground stone-lined tunnel associated with Iron Age settlements.
One theory is that they were built to store butter, cheese and other foodstuffs during the long winters.

Camas Ban on the track leading from Claigan to the Coral Beaches on a perfect day in late spring.

The fine white sand of the Coral Beaches is not true coral but comes from the bleached exoskeletons of the red seaweed *Lithothanium Calcareum*. The Coral Beaches are only accessible via the path from Claigan.

The Coral Beaches photographed after a winter of severe storm-force winds with gusts recorded locally of well over 100 mph, with some of the beach being deposited on to the foreshore giving an appearance of a light dusting of snow.

The small island of Lampay can be reached at low tide from the Coral Beaches. The settlements on the far shore are Husabost and Uig having the same name as the main port (some 14 miles north east from here) to the Outer Isles.

The bright white sands give an illusion of a tropical island when set against the deep blue sea on a sunny day.
The small island of Isay lies just offshore with cliffs rising steeply from the sea to a height of 90 ft.

The shells and seaweed have been arranged to create a picture.
But is it art ?

Left:
Cnoc Mor Ghrobain looking back toward Macleod's Table North. The cloud that appears beyond the mountain is in fact smoke from the controlled burning of the heather moorland that can benefit sheep and red deer. Know as the muirburn period it can extend in some highland areas until May when some birds have started nesting.

Sunlight reflecting on a small pool left on the Coral Beaches as the tide retreats.

Left:
Cnoc Mor Ghrobain affords splendid views south to Macleod's Tables, west to Dunvegan Head and
north-east to Waternish. A modest climb of 65 ft compared to Skye's other coastal features but well worth the effort.

Lovaig Bay and across to Stein on the coast and the scattered settlement of Lusta inland. Waternish the next destination a mere 2.5 miles across the sea. Due to the geography of Skye the journey by road is over 14 miles emphasising how Skye is made up of more than a dozen long sea lochs. This is mirrored in several locations on Skye making for some truly scenic coastal journeys.

Waternish

The road to Waternish begins at Fairy Bridge formerly the site of a cattle market. The road runs through Lusta then at a small junction drops down steeply to Stein on the shores of Loch Bay a distance of over 4 miles. The single track road continues for a further 3.5 miles to Trumpan. Beyond Trumpan is nothing but cliffs and moorland. A small track that can be very wet particularly after a spell of rain continues until it fades onto Waternish Point.

Stein nestling on the shores of Loch Bay is home to the oldest inn on Skye and affords the most spectacular sunsets with a magnificent backdrop across Loch Bay to the small island of Isay, Ardmore Point on Waternish and beyond to the Outer Hebrides. Stein was originally built as a fishing village complete with accommodation for the fisherman in the late 1700s, but it seemed that the settlers could survive on the land without having to spend time at sea.

As with many locations in the Highlands, Waternish has been the scene of several past clan battles. The ruined church at Trumpan was the scene in 1578 of the infamous massacre of several of Clan Macleod by the MacDonalds of Uist. The congregation were barricaded in the church by the MacDonalds who then set it alight; all perished except for a small girl who managed to escape to raise the alarm. Vengeance was swift by surviving members of Clan Macleod and the MacDonalds never sailed back to Uist.

It has been said that this is where Skye meets the sky and at times the Outer Hebrides that run in an arc for over 130 miles from south to north feel almost touchable, even though they are over 25 miles distant. A cairn on the track to Waternish Point (grid reference 230 632), built as a memorial to Roderick Macleod of Unish who died during clan battles with MacDonalds of Trotternish around 1530, bears witness to another battle. Unish was once a thriving settlement until the Highland Clearances, and all that remains are the sites of the ruined croft houses.

Legend has it that Bonnie Prince Charlie with the aid of Flora Macdonald, whilst escaping from South Uist after defeat at Culloden in 1746, landed near Waternish Point to rest. Eventually he sailed from Portree to safe refuge in France. The famous Skye Boat Song is said to be part of an old sea shanty.

Loch Bay from the shore at Stein. Stein was built in the 1780s as a fishing village complete with houses for the fisherman and a pier. For a while it became the busiest fishing village on Skye. Home at one time to the sixties singer Donovan, it is now a picturesque seaside village.

A fine end to a fine spring day at Stein with a spectacular sunset unfolding.

Above:
Stein Inn sign showing
the effects of salt water
spray on the shore of
Loch Bay.

Left:
The inn at Stein.

The Stein Inn is said to be
the oldest inn on Skye and was
built in the eighteenth century.
Many a sea shanty must have
been sung in the bar over the
last two hundred years.

The peat fire provides
a warm welcome.

A fascinating variety of vegetation can be spotted underfoot when walking across damp ground.

Left:
A close look at what is underfoot is something that can be easily overlooked on this truly scenic island. Violet (*Viola Riviniana*), generally the most common violet being unscented, appears from late March to May in woods, grassy places and on mountains.

Loch Bay from Stein with Dunvegan Head visible on the far shore.

Trumpan Old Church

Trumpan's place in history was earned by two massacres on the same day, a Sunday in May 1578.
What led to that terrible day stemmed from an attack that Clan Macleod carried out in 1577 during
a raid when almost 400 MacDonalds were killed on the Isle of Eigg. They were suffocated being
entrapped in a cave, the entrance then set alight by the Macleods.

On that Sunday in 1578 the MacDonalds from Uist having arrived at Ardmore Bay below Trumpan barricaded the
local population in the church, setting fire to the thatched roof. All of the congregation were killed apart from a
small girl who managed to escaped to raise the alarm.

Clan Macleod arrived swiftly to seek revenge and the MacDonalds never returned to Uist. Capturing the boats that by now were
stranded in Ardmore Bay as the tide had retreated, they attacked and killed the MacDonalds, then lined them up next to a turf dyke
which was pushed over burying their bodies. To this end the Battle of Trumpan is also referred to as the battle of the spoiled dyke.

The Waternish Peninsula affords the most spectacular of sunsets.

Left:
Beyond Trumpan there is nothing but cliffs and open moorland, but this has not always been so. This area was affected by the infamous Highland Clearances and all that is left now are the ruined crofts at Unish. The cairn was built as a memorial to Roderick Macleod of Unish who died during the clan battle around 1530 between the MacDonalds of Trotternish and the Macleods.

As the sun drops below the horizon the seascape takes on a magical appearance. Again across Loch Bay to Dunvegan Head.

Trotternish and the West Coast

A brief visit to Trotternish and the west coast

Trotternish is the largest of Skye's many peninsulas and boasts the spectacular Trotternish Ridge, an inland cliff that runs for almost 20 miles winding its way along the centre of the peninsula from Portree in the south to its northern end close to Staffin. It is home to the famous Quiraing. The ridge is crossed by the single track road at grid reference 439 679 from Staffin to Uig, a most scenic route with one particularly steep section close to the ridge.

The ridge is made up of pinnacles and peaks and steep cliff faces. Most notable of the pinnacles being Old Man of Storr grid reference 500 540 on the slopes of The Storr. The pinnacle is a spectacular sight that can be seen from many vantage points and stands 160 ft high undercut at the base. The Storr summit stands at over 2350 ft and is the highest point on the ridge. The Storr has featured in many television and film productions among these the 1975 film 'The Land That Time Forgot' and the television series 'Hamish Macbeth'.

Most of the ridge is easily accessible and with most of the walking on turf paths. The whole route can be walked in two days but the area can be treacherous with mists descending from nowhere that can last for several days.

The most northerly point on Skye culminates at Rubha Hunish with a steep decent from the cliffs to the headland that may not be suitable for some to attempt. The history of Trotternish is vast and varied, with the souterrain at Kilvaxter similar to Claigan as evidence of past civilisation whilst the Skye Museum of Island Life has a home at Kilmuir that recreates the croft settlements of the late 1800s.

Struan on the western coastline is home to Dun Beag Broch, one of Skye's many brochs, being Iron Age forts. Carbost on the shores of Loch Harport is home of the famous Talisker distillery built in 1830. Loch Harport is over 5 miles long and is the route to Glen Brittle a popular route into the Cuillin Hills.

Skye Museum of Island Life, Kilmuir. Seven thatched cottages depict the life of crofters from the nineteenth century.
On display are items used by Bonnie Prince Charlie and Flora Macdonald, items from clan battles and stone age axe heads.

Skye Museum of Island Life.

The Trotternish Ridge. Looking North along the ridge that runs for over 20 miles from Portree in the South to the famous Quiraing at the northern end. Although generally good walking mist often shrouds the summits.

An inland cliff. The ridge from the single track road that links Staffin to Uig the main port. The route crosses the ridge at grid reference 439 679 at a height of 840 ft with a particularly steep section close to the summit.

Winter on Skye. Storr lochs, Loch Fada and Loch Leathan at 446 ft lie below The Storr at over 2350 ft.

The Trotternish peninsula is the largest of Skye's many peninsulas and is home to Skye's most northerly point Rubha Hunish. The waterfall featured here flows into Loch Leathan at grid reference 494 510 on the road from Portree to Staffin. Portree takes its name from the Gaelic meaning 'King's Port', from a visit by King James V of Scotland in 1540 attempting to resolve the feuds between the local clans.

The Storr is the highest part of the Trotternish Ridge that runs for more than 20 miles.
The ridge is made up of more than a dozen peaks that can often be enveloped in cloud and mist.

The Old Man of Storr stands 165 ft high being undercut at the base. It was first climbed in 1955. It has featured as a backdrop in many film and television series.

Loch Harport on the west coast. Storm clouds gather looking very grey and
threatening from Gesto Bay toward Carbost and the distant Cuillin Hills.

A classic highland scene, cattle resting and boats at safe anchorage at the head of Loch Harport.

Right:
Highland cattle are said to be docile but I was glad to see the wire fencing on this occasion. The grey skies are becoming more threatening but still a glimmer of sun shines through.

Residents of Skye, first introduced in the eighteenth century.

Right:
One of many ancient forts on Skye, Dun Beag Broch near Struan overlooking Loch Bracadale.
In 1772 the author of *A Tour In Scotland,* Thomas Pennant, visited and wrote of the broch. Built for defence,
it is an Iron Age structure with two concentric stone walls one having a depth of 12 ft from ground level.

Early evening light on the Cuillin Hills viewed from Coire an-t Seasaich, a lone sheep looking on.

The Cuillins from Satran. The main ridge is over seven miles long comprising over 30 major peaks of which several are Munros. The striking feature here is the tall trees as Skye's interior is for the most part treeless bare moorland and windswept coast and mountains.

Sligachan

Sligachan lies at the foot of the Cuillin Hills, the correct name for the mountain range. However, this sounds somewhat more gentle than the reality of the magnificent ridges and peaks that have been described as the most untamed mountainous region in Britain. The range is made up of several Munros – being peaks above 3000 ft and named after Sir Hector Munro, an early leader of mountaineering in Scotland who set out to survey every peak above 3000 ft in 1891.

His aim was to climb them all and his last would have been in the summer of 1914 had he climbed The Inaccessible Pinnacle that was first conquered in 1880; alas, he never made it. Set high in the Cuillin Hills at a height over 3200 ft the pinnacle has vertical rock faces on three sides with the east ridge steep and exposed.

Sligachan Bridge, now replaced by a new road bridge, still stands proud. This area of Skye was a favourite spot of Alfred Wainwright who despite his vast reference works on the Lake District always spent his holidays north of the border with Skye one of his preferred destinations.

Glen Sligachan is the most favoured route into the Cuillin for many of the high level routes. These should only be undertaken when fully prepared and experienced although the lower slopes also provide some breathtaking mountain views and rewarding experiences without too much difficulty.

A classic mountain view is afforded from the bridge at Sligachan with the almost text-book mountain of Marsco over 2350 ft standing out with the higher peaks in the background. Marsco is a fairly straightforward ascent although steep when compared to the more loftier regions that require a great deal of scrambling on the upper slopes.

Loch Sligachan is fed by the River Sligachan that rises high above Harta Corrie, cascading some 7 miles to the bridge then flowing a further 3 miles as Loch Sligachan to the sea.

A perfect winter's day. Sunshine glistening on the snow-capped peaks of Marsco standing just over 2350 ft and
Garbn Bheinn beyond at over 2500 ft. Above and beyond the leaning electricity pole are the slopes of Druim na Ruaige.

Marsco this time viewed from the south with the lower slopes of Bla Bheinn in the foreground.

Right:
Marsco on an overcast day towers above Glen Sligachan. A relatively straightforward hill walk
on grassy and boggy slopes with very little scree unlike the higher peaks.

Skye Mountain Rescue, Sligachan.
The Skye mountain rescue team has two main bases located at Sligachan and
Glenbrittle built with the generous help of the Order of St John.
The base stations are used during rescue operations by the 35-strong volunteers
who provide assistance to walkers and climbers in difficulty on Skye.

Left:
Glen Sligachan is the most popular route into the Cuillin Hills. These are the most dangerous
mountains in Britain and the highest peaks should only be attempted by experienced climbers.
The River Sligachan rises high on the slopes of Harta Corrie.

Ben Tianavaig at just over 1330 ft towers over the island's capital Portree to the north with its colourful harbour. Taken near Sconser, Loch Sligachan. A single track road runs from Peinmore near Portree to Peinchorran one of the settlements on the opposite side of the loch. Just under a half a mile across the loch, the journey by road from this point is a staggering 17 miles. Ben Tianavaig grid reference 511 410. The Trotternish Ridge can be clearly seen.

Left:
The Cuillin Hills from the road to Dunvegan at Sligachan. Am Bhasteir and Bhasteir Tooth can be seen beyond the ridge with the summit of Sgurr a Bhasteir just 100 ft short of Munro status.

Skye Sunset

Late evening across Loch Pooltiel. In June Skye enjoys long hours of daylight as
the sun sets just below the horizon around midnight to rise just a few hours later.

Looking across Loch Bay, Waternish to the Outer Isles

On the shores of Stein with Dunvegan Head clearly visible.

Loch Harport. The evening sky and the loch had taken on a lustre of pink and pale blue.

The unmistakable tops of Healabhal Mhor and Healabhal Bheag. Macleod's Tables viewed this time from the south east near Loch Harport are a dominant feature of the Duirinish peninsula, contributing to a most striking sunset.